THE INSPIRED AUTHORING

CHANGE

EMMANUEL ERIM

CHANGE

EMMANUEL ERIM

TABLE OF CONTENTS

DEDICATION

I specially dedicate this book to my Late Father, Late Mr. Otioh, Ankpo Erim and to my Great Mother, Eld. Mrs. Justina Erim.

ACKNOWLEDGEMENT

I appreciate God for the series of inspirations through which this book has reached its peak.

I also appreciate the Great Enerst Shuttleff Holmes who's "Creative Mind and Success" has contributed immensely to the propagation of this version of his inspired authoring.

As you read ahead, if carefully completed, you will experience 75% change in your general understanding of life, insentiently. This change will surely unleash the real you.

INTRODUCTION

The most mysterious event of life is change, change is either positive or negative, and everything in the world is experiencing change. As insignificant as an element of change it will surely manifest a significant change. Change in all definition is a gradual differentiation with time, which can be traced or noticed.

Change existed in the very beginning of things, and still exist now, we can say that the creation were changes resulting from the commands from the Creator. The command is the action and the result became a change noticeable as creation. Change is continuous and will keep occurring which means that creation is continuous, as the sun's shadow shifts, so there is no permanence on earth. Everything comes to pass, nothing comes to stay, and nothing remains constant except change itself.

Change is the result of a new action. All change is not growth, as all movement is not forward. While all changes do not lead to improvement, all improvement requires change which is why change could be either positive or negative. The ability to develop, test, and implement changes is essential for any individual that wants to continuously improve.

To change means to add to, remove from or make a new one, which implies the same as to create. Whoever has the ability to create, solely, has the ability to change what is created. Everything which exists today was created; we learn that in the beginning when there was nothing, creation started that means change started right from the beginning, everything we see today came as a result of change or creation. The Creator is the only one to continue creation and changing the world without limit to where, how and what to.

THE CREATOR

Let's discover who the Creator is; the Creator is a very sophisticated being. In the hierarchy of power,

Almighty God is the most powerful, followed by the Creator. The Creator created the heavens and the earth, the earth was formless and empty, and darkness was over the surface of the deep. The Creator went ahead and created the light and separated it from the darkness, created land and separated it from the waters, created vegetation on the land and aquatic creatures, created the sun, moon and the stars.

Who is now the Creator? This is the question in your mind, but let me hint you. There is no significant difference between Almighty God and the Creator. The Creator is the centre of God in God, the Creator can also be considered as God's companion, being made to be like God. You can now make right deductions of who the Creator is, let's now discover the Creator.

The Creator is man. This book is going to be driving on the sub-theme “The Hidden Power of Man”. The Almighty God is not and has no intensions to being the Creator which the truth of nature reveals, creation power is given only to man, to create and change the entire universe without any limit. God only assumed the position of the Creator so as to create a few things that will make man comfortable in a way of showing example to man on what he should do, but after God created man, he stopped creating because creation is not the duty of God but of man, he made man to become the Creator and continue from where He stopped. Which means that; man is occupying the same office which created the Heavens and the Earth, and which makes man capable of changing and creating anything, all that man needs to do is to understand the truth which is the truth of nature.

Therefore it follows that man, too, is made out of God, since God is all. And as a result, he must partake of God's nature, for we are "made in His image." Man is a center of God in God. Whatever God is universally, man must be in his individual world.

God made man to live with Him, to be one with the Father. Indeed, it is true that those who have felt this most deeply have had a resultant spiritual power that leads us to suppose that God really did make man as a companion. "As the Father hath life within Himself, so hath he given it to the man to have life within himself." Man's mind is made out of God's mind, and all that man is or ever will be, all that he has or ever will have, must partake of the God's nature. Man did not make it so, but it is so, and he must accept the fact and see what he can do with it.

Having the same power in his individual life that God has in the Universal, then this unearthing will imply liberty from all servitude when he understands the truth of nature. As God oversees His Universal world so will man govern his individual world, always subject to the greater law and life. God governs not through physical law as result, but first by inner knowing - then the physical follows. In the same way, man governs his world by the process which we will call, for want of a better name, the power of his thought. Man's inner life is one with the Father.

There is no separation, for the self-evident reason that there is nothing to separate him from God, because there is nothing but life. The separation of two things implies putting a different element between them; but as there is nothing different from God, the unity of God and man is established forever. "My Father and I are One" is a simple statement of a great soul who perceived life as it really is and not from the mere standpoint of outer conditions. Taking as the starting point that man has the same life as God, it follows that he uses the same creative process and changing ability. Everything is one, comes from the same source and returns again to it. "The things which are seen are not made of the things which do appear." What we see comes from what we do not see.

This explains the observable universe, and is the only possible explanation. As God's thought makes worlds and peoples in them with all living things, so does our thought make our world and peoples it with all the understandings we have had. By the activity of our thought things come into our life, and we are limited because we have not known the truth; we have thought that outside things controlled us, when all the time we have had that within which could have changed everything and given us freedom from bondage.

Why did God create man and make him a free agent? Isn't this the question in your mind? If God had created us to conform to, or to be anything that was not of our will, we should not have had individuality at all, we should be automatons. Since we know that we are individuals, we know that God made us thus; and we are just discovering the reason why. Let any man realize this, the greatest truth in all ages, and he will find it will answer all questions. He will be satisfied that things are what they are. He will perceive that he may use his own God-given power so to work, to think and to live that he will in no way hinder the greater law from operating through him.

According to the clearness of his perception and the greatness of his realization of this truth will he provide within himself a starting point through which he may operate. There will no longer be a sense of separation, but in its place will come that divine assurance that he is one with God, and thus will he find his freedom from all suffering, whether it be of body, mind or estate.

The Creator has been revealed to be Man, and Man has ever since inception been fully involved in creation.

Man has everything it takes to create whatever man wants, as good Creator as God was, so is man. Man is so equipped enough to create a planet into existence, God has shown man all level of humility and love by allowing man to have all the tools of creation that He possesses which makes man an efficient creator just as God was. The truth of nature says that God created man in His own image and likeness, God had to do this in order for man to be fit enough to be in companion with Him.

The whole universe is waiting and willing to conform to whatever the Creator wants of it. Man being the only Creator as God has made him reserves the power to create and change the entire universe.

Whoever created a computer software/application reserves the right in the form of a source code through which more creation and changes may be effected on the said software/application, except the owner decides to handover the copyrights or source code to another person, which is what was done between God and man. God has given man the right to subdue the earth and he remains the only one with the tools of creation which makes him the only Creator. The Creator of the universe reserves the power and legal right to change the universe; therefore, man alone has the power to change his world.

The power which the Creator uses for creation comes from his ability to understand the truth, any man that lacks understanding of the truth, lacks the creative ability and ceases from his position as the Creator, only men who understand the truth do change the world, add to creation and lead a successful life. Living successfully in this case implies; man's ability to fulfill the purpose for which he existed, man is supposed to dominate and subdue all the creation. The greatest joy of God is in seeing man understand the truth, live by it and fulfill his purpose.

Every man is a completed project, in other words, God Almighty owes man nothing, and man has in him everything he wants, the love of God for man has been perfected by giving man access to God's Divine Nature. Man needs to know the truth, everything we want is in Him and we have every access to the truth. The fall of man came as a result of ignorance; ignorance remains the greatest weak point of every living man, the advantage which the devil used against man in the beginning was his knowledge of the truth which man was ignorant of. Therefore, the way forward, if man must resume his place as the Creator is to embrace knowledge and forsake ignorance.

WHAT BRINGS ABOUT CHANGE?

NEEDS

All the created things were created as a result of need, which means, everything that was created is needful and important to the world. While needs are universal, desires or wants are temporal, spatial, and personal. Thus, desires can be or actually are manipulated by perverted applications of needs approaches. If this distinction is acceptable, the term 'needs' would stand for general principles of human existence.

Have you ever wondered the importance of some creatures to nature or to the Creator; you need to first understand that everything created by the Creator was created for the Creator's use. Now let's see it from this scenario; the Creator was mean to own the world and everything created and to create more things according to his needs. Also, the Creator is supposed to according to his will change whatever is created to suite his needs. Therefore, seeing needs is one activity which qualifies one to be called Creator, the Creator as implied by this book is another version of man, meaning; a fulfilled version of man. In the circular world they are referred to as leaders, legends in their respective fields, great men, successful men, and so on.

The major factor that is behind and which inspires and drives the Creator into creating anything is need. The ability to conceive a burden or need in heart is always the first step to invention, change and creation. Seeing a need gives you an avenue to ask and we get in life what we have the courage to ask for.

Change begins within, you can change the entire universe just by changing one thing in you, everyone thinks of changing the world, but no one thinks of changing himself. When we are no longer able to change a situation, we are challenged to change ourselves. Conceive a burden and the world stands the risk of changing again.

IDEAS

Conception of new ideas is another factor which brings about change, if an idea is conceived and appreciated; it has the potency to manifest as change. Therefore, conceiving an idea about any realized need which you want to solve is another step taken to ensure change. When you are fed with ideas which are picked up for discussion, exchanged, altered and repeated, or discarded. Ideas get the discourse off the ground and make up its core nourishment.

Though creating ideas is actually a thought process which takes some form in the mind before becoming a reality. There is certainly nothing unsystematic about generating ideas. Some start out in a fantasy form only to be fine-tuned into creating something functional and practical.

If you dream of ever being great, then one thing you should treasure most is ideas, this is what rules the world, this is what makes the rich, and it's a great determinant of success. Inspired ideas are generated in the mind, for creative purpose.

CRITERIA TO MAKE A CHANGE

CHARISMA

There are some qualities which are common among world changers; we shall discuss them in this session. Let's start with the first being charisma, making change in all aspect of life is the hobby of charismatic people, throughout my career I have often found myself in the company of individuals who have that indefinable quality that draws you to them, and leaves you feeling wonderfully energised as a result of meeting them.

Charismatic people became my passion. I paid attention to the way Charismatic people spoke, how they moved, their posture and the type of words they used. The more I noticed the more confused I became about being able to categorise the elements that typify this level of intensive magnetism.

Consequently, I was a victim of an eventual change which came as a result of my involvement with a very charismatic young man. Late In the month of December, 2018, I saw an adverts flyer in Diamond Bank as I went to deposit, I picked interest in meeting the team offering the services as it was in my field (IT Services). They were offering website development & business starters' packages. Two weeks after I contacted them I was lucky to meet with the Chief Executive Officer at Mr. Fans in Calabar, Cross River State of Nigeria.

Before I go any further with how meeting this young man influenced, affected and obviously change me in many ways, let me sound a piece of advice; we all have to be careful with the kind of people we set out for our lives or get attracted to for they have a way of influencing and changing us.

The young man remains anonymous; I loved his approach, the way he spoke, laughed, dressed, walked and everything about him was interesting. He offered me to be a member of his team after several hours of conversation. After a while he invited me to their team meeting, introduced me and offered to be paying me to work for the team as a website developer. As time went on he discovered that I was good in it and had to hand over a very important project of his team to me, and he made me the director of ICT in the team.

Before now, I had a female friend who travelled out of town; she stayed for a month and came back. On meeting me, she stared at me for more than it was necessary and was saying that I have really changed in the way I walked, spoke, laughed and so on. She became very eager to know the secret behind the change, I personally knew the secret, I equally knew when I began changing in the way I spoke and laughed but I couldn't help or prevent it because of how much I really wished to be like him in my mind. Those thought of being like him started manifesting automatically without me doing anything to enhance those changes.

Anything you take to heart has a way of becoming part of you including the people you set out for your live. Charisma is one quality you must possess if you must affect, influence and change your world.

Charismatic people possess a potent blend of attractiveness and presence that commands attention with an irresistible magnetic force.

According to studies of babies and infants by Judith Langlois of the University of Texas, in experimental studies attractive people earn more and progress further in their careers. A Charismatic person doesn't have to be physically attractive to possess the power to attract. Attractiveness is hard wired in our brains and stimulates a primeval reaction from others that 'attractive means they are healthier and have better breeding potential.' When we meet or observe a Charismatic person we are attracted to their aura of 'special-ness', believing that their 'special-ness' could overspill into our own personality, infecting us, as if by osmosis, with a magical presence.

As with all power, possessing Charisma brings with it great responsibility; as you get to grips with the profound ways you can develop and strengthen your Charisma you'll experience an increase in your personal power. If you use this power with positive intent for others you will be acting from an inner platform of compassion and integrity that will serve to electrify your presence to the next stage. Charisma is a must trait for all world changers, you must possess it if you must affect and change your world.

HOW TO DEVELOP CHARISMA

Life is 10% what happens to us and 90% how we react to it. Any man who knows how to love everybody, no matter who they are, will find ample of people who will return that love to him. This is not mere mawkishness, and it is more than a religious attitude of mind; it is a deep scientific fact, and one to which we should pay attention. The reason is this: As all is mind, and as we attract to us what we first become, until we learn to love we are not sending out love vibrations, and not until we send out love vibrations can we receive love in return.

The first thing to do is to learn to love everybody. If you have not done this, begin now. There is always more good than bad in people, and seeing the good tends to bring it forth. Love is the greatest healing and drawing power on earth. It is the very cause for our being, and that elucidates why it is that people should have something or somebody to love. The life that has not loved has not lived; it is still dead. Love is the sole impulse for creation; and the man who does not have it as the greatest incentive in his life has never developed the real creative instinct.

The whole universe is established upon love. The atmosphere created by a real lover of the race is so powerful that although, his other shortcomings may be many, still the world will love him in return. "To him who loves much, much will be given." People are dying for real human interest, for someone to tell them that they are all right. Which people do we like the better: the one who is always full of trouble and faultfinding, or the one who looks at the world as his friend and loves it? The question does not need to be asked; we know that we want the company of the person who loves and loving, forgets all else. The only reason we think other people are "queer" is because they do not happen to think as we do. We must get over this little, petty attitude and see things in the large. The person who sees what he wants to see, regardless of what appears, will someday experience in the outer what he has so faithfully seen within.

From egoistic reasons alone, if from no loftier reason, we cannot afford to find fault or to hate or even to hold in mind anything against any living soul. The God who is love cannot hear the prayer of the man who is not love. Love and cooperation will yet be found to be the greatest business principle on earth. "God is Love." We will make our unity with all people, with all life. We will affirm that God in us is unified with God in all. This One is now drawing into our life all love and fellowship. I am one with all people, with all things, with all life. As I listen in the silence the voice of all humanity speaks to me and answers the love that I hold out to it. This great love that I now feel for the world is the love of God, and it is felt by all and returned from all. Nothing comes in between because there is nothing but love to come in between.

I understand all people and that understanding is reflected back to me from all people. I help, therefore I am helped. I uplift, therefore I am uplifted. Nothing can mar this perfect picture of myself and my relations with the world; it is the truth, the whole truth, and nothing but the truth. I am now surrounded by all love, all friendship, all companionship, all health, all happiness, and all success. I am one with life. I wait in the silence while the Great Spirit bears this message to the whole world.

GAIN INDEPENDENCE

God gave us the gift of life; it is up to us to give ourselves the gift of living well. Life isn't about finding yourself, life is about creating yourself. Never depend on other people. You have strength of your own that is great enough to create a very wonderful world around you. The Almighty has implanted a mastermind within the soul of everyone and what we need to do is to unearth that inner genius and cause it to shine forth.

We will never do this while we look to others for direction. “To thine own self repair, wait thou within the silence dim, and thou shalt find Him there.” All the power and intelligence of the Universe is already within, waiting to be utilized. Self-reliance is the word to abide on. Listen to your own voice; it will speak in terms that are unmistakable.

Belief in your own self more than in all else, all great men have learned to do this. Every person, within his own soul, is in direct communication with the Infinite Understanding. When we depend on other people we are simply taking their light and trying to light our path with it. When we depend on ourselves we are depending on that inner voice that is God, speaking in and through man. “Man is the inlet and the outlet to all there is in God." God has made us and brought us up to where we recognize our own individuality; from now on we will have to let Him express through us. If it were different we should not be individuals. "Behold I stand at the door and wait." This is a statement of the near presence of power; but we, the Individual, must open the door. This door is our thought and we are the guardian of it, and when we do open the door we will find that the Divine Presence is right at hand, waiting, ready and willing to do for us all that we can believe. We are strong with the strength of the Infinite. We are not weak. We are great and not mean. We are one with the Infinite Mind.

When you have a real thing to do, keep it to yourself, don't talk about it. Just know in your own mind what it is that you want and keep still about it. Often when we think that we will do some big thing we begin to talk about it and the first thing we know all the power seems to be gone.

This is what happens. We are all sending out into Mind a constant stream of thought; the clearer it is the better will it manifest; if it becomes doubtful it will not have so clear a manifestation. If it is confused it will manifest only confusion. When you want to do a big thing, get the mental pattern, make it perfect, know just what it means, enlarge your thought, keep it to yourself, pass it over to the creative power behind all things, wait and listen, and when the impression comes, follow it with assurance. Don't talk to anyone about it. Never listen to negative talk or pay any attention to it and you will succeed where all others fail. It takes one man to change the entire universe, it takes only you to create everything your mind can conceive, your mind cannot conceive more than it can execute, so you do not need assistance from anyone to accomplish your dreams.

Hard work entails having the strength to do a thing and the perseverance to continue until success is achieved. The most beautiful people I've known are those who have known trials, have known struggles, have known loss, and have found their way out of the depths. Strength does not come from winning. Your struggles develop your strengths. When you go through hardships and decide not to surrender, that is strength. Being hard working is the edge that successful people have over others.

Everyone wants to be successful. Of course, your definition of success can and should be different - because success should mean something different to each of us - but still, we all want to succeed at whatever we choose to do. (Otherwise, why do it?) But whenever I give a thought to how success is often based on outworking other people - both in terms of effort and in terms of hours spent - I get indignant responses. “What about work-life balance?” some ask.

"Work smarter, not harder," others say. Yeah, well, no way.

You can't have it both ways. On the one hand, we celebrate people who have worked incredibly hard and achieved incredible success. They're icons, world changers and are putting in enough to be the Creator which God made them. Take successful entrepreneurs. Bill Gates evidently never slept, never changed clothes, never did anything but code and manoeuvre and strategise. In an industry filled with incredibly smart people – where smart was and is commonplace – he rose to the top by also working incredibly hard.

Mark Cuban didn't take a vacation for seven years while he started his first company. Elon Musk says, "You just have to put in 80- to 100-hour weeks every week. If other people are putting in 40-hour workweeks and you're putting in 100hour workweeks, then, even if you're doing the same thing, you know that you will achieve in four months what it takes them a year to achieve." In fact, the common theme of almost every tale of entrepreneurial success is a person who worked countless 18- to 24-hour days. Replace the names and their stories sound almost identical. Even Tim Ferriss, the lord of the four hour-workweek manor, stays incredibly busy with all his projects. (Of course, to Tim it doesn't feel like work.) Or take successful people in other professions.

Jeffrey Immelt, the chief executive of GE, worked 100-hour weeks for 24 years. In a company filled with incredibly driven people - where incredible drive is commonplace - he rose to the top by also working incredibly hard. Tim Cook of Apple still wants to be first in, last out. Or take sports. Hard work has clearly paid off for all of them. Yet somehow people think hard work won't work for them. Maybe that's because of the whole "work smarter" thing? Successful people already work smarter.

They don't work mindlessly or inefficiently or ineffectively.

Where success is concerned, working smarter is a given. Extremely successful people work smarter and they work harder. Their effort is heroic, their payoff is often legendary, and we celebrate them for it. "Wait," you say. "Luck plays a big part in success. So, does timing. So, do a lot of other factors." You're right. But you can't control luck. You can't always control timing. You can't always control all those other factors. What can you always control? How hard you work. Let's say luck decides to pay everyone with a particular amount which you cannot control, what is going to set the difference and keep you outstanding is the extra effort you put. Again, everyone defines success differently, as well everyone should.

You may not be smarter than everyone else. You may not be as talented. You may not have the same great connections, the same great environment, or the same great education. If you're on the downside of advantage, you may have none of those things. But you can always rely on your courage, your effort, and your perseverance.

You can always substitute effort for skill and experience, secure in the knowledge that, over time, incredible effort will absolutely breed skill and experience. You can always, always, always work harder than everyone else. Want to be different? Hard work can be your immediate difference. Make hard work your favourite words, whether at work or at home or in your marriage or wherever your definition of success takes you. That way you'll never have to look back and wonder what you might have accomplished if only you had tried harder.

The most significant life lesson I have learned from working with Registered Holsteins is that hard work leads to success. Whether you want a political office, entrepreneurial success, marital success, academic success, or whatever you want to change in your world, hard work is inevitable. Keep striving and working harder because there are many ways of going forward, but only one way of standing still.

FAITH

All of the great inventions in the world have been accomplished by people who have kept on trying when there seemed to be no hope at all.

Faith is necessary always when we want something we must believe. Faith is not in asking for something but it is in believing that we already have the things that we need. This already-believing is necessary because all is mind, and until we have provided that full acceptance, we have not made a mold into which mind could pour itself and through which it could manifest.

In the previous chapters, we made mentioned that man has access to God's Divine Nature, through which the heavens and the earth was created. God made man to be the Creator of all things including what is considered impossible that man can make anything through faith.

This positive belief is absolutely essential to real creative work; and if we do not at present have it, then we must develop it. All is law, and cause and effect obtain through all life. Mind is cause, and what we term matter, or the visible, is effect. As water will freeze into the form that it is poured, so mind will solidify only into the forms that our thought takes. Thought is form. The individual provides the form; he never creates or even manifests, – that is, of himself; there is something that does all this for him. His sole activity is the use of this power.

This authority is always at hand ready to be spoken into and at once ready to form the words into visible expression. But the mold that most of us provide is a very poor one, and we change it so quickly that it is more like a motion picture than anything else. Already we have the power; it is the gift of the Most High in its Finite Expression. But our ignorance of its use has caused us to create the wrong form, which in its turn has caused mind to produce the form which we have thought into it. From this truth of nature or law of cause and effect we may never hope to escape; and while we may think of it as a hard thing, at first, yet, when we understand, we shall see it as absolute justice without which there could be no real self-acting, individual life at all.

Because of our divine individuality, even God may have to wait our recognition of the truth. People in business will do well to remember this and so to form their thought that they will be willing to receive what they send out. No thought of discouragement or disorder should ever be created, but only positive assurance, strong thoughts of success, of Divine activity, the feeling that through understanding the truth of nature all things are possible, the belief that we are One with that Great Mind. These are the thoughts that make for success. The realization that we are dealing with one and not with two powers enables us to think with clearness.

We are not troubled about competition or opposition or failure because there is nothing but life, and this life is continually giving to us all that we could ask for, wish, or think into it. We can now see how essential it is that thought should be held one-pointed; that we should think always and only upon what we want, never letting our mind dwell on anything else. In this way the Spirit works through us.

Faith is the only currency that is a legal tender and accepted across the globe. When money fails, faith never fails. It's only faith that can draw from the reserves of Heaven. Faith comes by revelation; the truth of nature says "So then faith cometh by hearing, and hearing and understanding the truth." The first level is reading, the second level is revelation.

What Is Faith? It is putting the truth to work. Taking steps on the truth you have learned. Obeying the truth of nature to prove that you believe in the Divine Nature, redemption is a call to profitable living.

NATURE'S DEBT STATUS

Nature is not and will never be indebted to the Creator; nature pays the Creator exactly what the Creator banks within it. Nature was created by and subjected to the Creator and at such cannot disobey the Creator; everything that The Creator has is what he has created into and through nature. The Creator only needs an understanding of the truth in order to manipulate nature; the same degree of the power of creation which existed is still in existence.

TOOLS FOR CHANGE/CREATION

THE TRUTH OF NATURE

Never does nature say one thing and wisdom another. Therefore knowing the truth about nature is having wisdom. The Creator must realize that he has life within himself as the great gift of God to him. If he really has life, if it is the same nature as the life of God, if he is an individual and has the right of self-choice which constitutes individuality; then it follows that he can do with his life what the wants to do: he can make out of Himself that which he wishes. Liberty is his, but this liberty is within law and never outside it, the law is the truth of nature. The Creator must have understanding of the truth.

The Creator is always in immediate connection with the Infinite of understanding. We are immersed in a living intelligence; we are surrounded by a Power that knows, for "In Him we live and move and have our being." If our outer thought were never confused, we should at all times draw from this Infinite source of knowledge; we should be guided by It and never make mistakes; our minds would be like the smooth surface of a lake, unruffled by wind and storm.

The truth of nature is the Word of God through which creation was perfected, the one important tool through which creation was established is the Word of God which is the truth of nature. In the beginning was the word and the word was with God and the word was God, He was in the beginning with God, all things were made through Him and without Him nothing was made that was made.

The most efficient tool of creation remains the word of truth, the truth of nature which is in God and has been revealed to be God. Therefore, knowing the truth is same as knowing God, having faith in the truth is also having faith in God. This tool is for creation and has been handed over to the Creator, that through it, the Creator shall fulfill His purpose.

The Creator's word, spoken forth through creative mind, is endowed with power of manifestation. "By our words we are justified and by our words we are condemned." Our word has the exact amount of power that we put into it. This does not mean power through effort or strain but power through absolute conviction, or faith. It is like a little messenger who knows what he is doing and knows just how to do it. We speak into our words the intelligence which we are, and backed by that greater intelligence of the Universal Mind our word becomes a law unto the thing for which it is spoken.

If any word has power it means that all words have power. Some words may have more power than others, according to our faith, but all words have some power. How careful, then, we should be what kind of words we are speaking for creation is perfected through the words of the Creator.

All this goes to prove that we really are one with the Infinite Mind, and that our words have the power of life within them; that the word is always with us and never far off. The word is within our own mouth. Every time we speak we are using power, we are creating and changing the world. We are one in mind with the whole universe; we are all eternally united in this mind with real power. It is our own fault if we do not use this truth after we see it. We should feel ourselves surrounded by this mind, this great pulsating life, this all-seeing and all-knowing reality.

When we do feel this near presence, this great power and life, then all we have to do is to speak forth into it, speak with all the positive conviction of the soul that has found its source, and above all else never fear but that it will be done unto us even as we have believed. What wonderful power, what a newness of life and of power of expression, is waiting for those who really believe. What may the race not attain to when men wake up to the real facts of being? As yet the race has not begun to live, but the time is drawing near. Already thousands are using this great power, and thousands are eagerly watching and waiting for the new day.

Understanding wisdom is the key. Wisdom is in the truth of nature, so, and understanding natural truth is having wisdom. An inquiry into Truth is an inquiry into the cause of things as the human race sees and experiences them. The truth of nature is a very important tool for creation and the Creator must acknowledge this for all level of efficiency.

THE MIND

The mind is the centre of it all and the starting point of our thought must always begin with our understandings. We all know that life is, else we could not even think that we are. Since we can think, say and feel we must be. We live, we are conscious of life; therefore we must be and life must be. If we are life and mindfulness (self-knowing) then it means that we must have come from life and mindfulness. Let us start, then, with this simple fact: Life is and life is conscious.

But what is the nature of this life; is it physical, mental, material or spiritual? A little careful thinking based upon logic, more than any merely personal opinion, will do much in clearing up some of these questions that at first seem to stagger us with their bigness. How much of that which is may we call life? The answer would have to be: Life is all that there is; it is the reason for all that we see, hear, feel-- all that we experience in any way.

Now nothing from nothing leaves anything, and it is impossible for something to proceed from nothing. Since something is, that from which it came must be all that is. Life, then, is all that there is. Everything comes from it, we included. The next question is, how do things come from life? How do the things that we see come from the things that we do not see? The things that we see must be real because we see them. To say they are not real will never explain them nor answer any question about them. God's world is not a world of illusion but one of divine realities. The truth must not explain away things that we see.

It must explain what they are. We are living and experiencing varying degrees of consciousness and conditions. Only when the why of this living and of our experiences is understood will we know the least thing about the truth.

OUR LIFE IS A RESULT OF OUR THINKING

It is easy for the ordinary person to see how it is that mind can control, and to a certain extent govern, the functions of the body. Some can go even further than this and see that the body is governed entirely by mindfulness. This they can see without much difficulty, but it is not so easy for them to see how it is that thought governs their conditions and decides whether they are to be successes or failures. Here we will stop to ask the question: If our conditions are not controlled by thought, by what, then, are they controlled? Some will say that conditions are controlled by circumstances. But what are circumstances? Are they "cause" or are they "effect?" Of course they are always effect; everything that we see is an effect. An effect is something that follows a cause, and we are dealing with causation only; effects do not make themselves, but they are held in place by mind, or causation.

If this does not answer your thought, begin over again and realize that behind everything that is seen is the silent cause. In your life you are that cause. There is nothing but mind, and nothing moves except as mind moves it. We have agreed that, while God is love, yet your life is governed absolutely by mind, or law. In our lives of conditions we are the cause, and nothing moves except as our mind moves it. The activity of our mind is thought. We are always acting because we are always thinking.

At all times we are either drawing things to us or we are pushing them away from us. In the ordinary individual this process goes on without his ever knowing it consciously, but ignorance of the law will excuse no one from its effects. "What?" someone will say, "Do you think that I thought failure or wanted to fail?" Of course not. You would be foolish to think that; but according to the law which we cannot deny, you must have thought things that would produce failure. Perhaps you thought that failure might come, or in some other way you gave it entrance to your mind.

Thinking back over the reason for things, you will find that you are surrounded by a mind, or law that casts back at the thinker manifested, everything that he thinks. If this were not true, the Creator would not be an individual. Individuality can mean only the ability to think what we want to think. If that thought is to have power in our lives then there has to be something that will manifest it.

No matter what we may do, law will always obtain. If we are thinking of ourselves as poor and needy, then mind has no choice but to return what we have thought into it. At first this may be hard to realize, but the truth will reveal to the seeker that law could act in no other way.

Whatever we think is the pattern, and mind is the builder. The Master, realizing this law, said, "It is done unto you even as you have believed." Shall we doubt but that this great Way Shower knew what he was talking about? Did He not say, "It is done unto you"? What a wonderful thought. "It is done unto you." Nothing to worry about. "It is done unto you." With a tremendous grasp of the power of true spiritual thought, the Master even called forth bread from the ethers of life, and at no time did He ever fail to demonstrate that when one knows the truth he is freed by that knowledge.

Is it any wonder that the truth of nature says, "With all thy getting get understanding"? The Master understood all this, and so it was no more effort for Him to do what He did than it is for us to breathe or to digest our food. He understood, that is all, because the Master did understand and did use these great laws with objective mindfulness.

The Creator uses creative power that already is. Relatively speaking, he is the creative power in his own life; and so far as his thought goes, there is something that goes with it that has the power to bring forth into manifestation the thing thought of. Hitherto we have used this creative power in ignorance and so have brought upon ourselves all kinds of conditions, but today hundreds of thousands are beginning to use these great laws of their being in a conscious, constructive way. Herein lies the great secret of the New Thought movements under their various names and cults and orders.

All are using the same law even though some deny to others the real revelation. We should get into an attitude of mind wherein we should recognize the truth wherever we may find it. The trouble with most of us is that unless we see sugar in a sugar bowl we think it must be something else, and so we stick to our petty prejudices instead of looking after principles.

WHAT TO DO FIRST

The first thing to realize is that since any thought manifests it means that all thought does the same, else how should we know that the particular thought we were thinking would be the one that would create? Mind must cast back all or none. Just as the creative power of the soil receives all seeds put into it, and at once begins to work upon them, so mind must receive all thought and at once begin to operate upon it. Thus we find that all thought has some power in our lives and over our conditions.

We are making our situations by the creative power of our thought. This atmosphere decides what is to be drawn to it. For instance, you never saw a successful man who went around with an atmosphere of failure. Successful people think about success. A successful man is filled with that understated something which permeates everything that he does with an atmosphere of confidence and strength. In the presence of some people we feel as though nothing were too great to undertake; we are hoisted; we are inspired to do great things, to accomplish; we feel strong, steady, sure. What a power we feel in the presence of big souls, strong men, and noble women! Did you ever stop to inquire why it is that such persons have this kind of an effect over you while others seem to depress, to drag you down, and in their presence you feel as though life were a weight to carry? One type is positive, the other negative. In every physical respect they are just alike, but one has a mental and spiritual power which the other does not have, and without that power the individual can hope to do but little.

Which of these two do we like most? With which do we want to associate? Certainly not with the one that depresses us; we have enough of that already. What about the man who inspires us with our own value? He remains the man we will turn to every time. Before ever we reach him, in our haste to be near, even to hear his voice, do we not feel a strength coming to meet us? Do you think that this man who has such a wonderful power of attraction will ever want for friends? Will he ever have to look up a position? Already so many positions are open to him that he is weighing in his mind which one to take. He does not have to become a success; he already is a success. Thoughts of failure, limitation or poverty are negative and must be counted out of our lives for all time. Somebody will say, "But what of the poor; what are you going to do with them; are they to be left without help?" No; a thousand times no. The same power is in them that is in all men. They will always be poor until they awake and realize what life is. All the charity on earth has never done away with poverty, and never will; if it could have done so it would have done so; it could not, therefore it has not.

It will do a man a thousand times more good to show him how to succeed than it will to tell him he needs charity. We need not listen to all the catastrophe howlers. Let them howl if it does them any good. God has given us the power to create more and change our world and we must use it. We can do more toward saving the world by proving this law than all that charity has ever given it. Right here, in the manifold world today, there is more money and provision than the world can use. Not even a fraction of the wealth of the world is used. Inventors and discoverers are adding to this wealth every day; they are the real people, the great men, the Creators, etc. But in the midst of plenty, surrounded by all the gifts of heaven, man sits and begs for his daily bread. He should be taught to realize that he has brought these conditions upon himself; that instead of blaming God, man or the devil for the circumstances by which he is surrounded, he should learn to seek the truth, to let the dead bury their dead.

We should tell every man who will believe what his real nature is; show him how to overcome all limitations; give him courage; show him the way. If he will not believe, if he will not walk in the way, it is not our fault, and having done all we can, we must go our way. We may sympathize with people but never with trouble, limitation or misery. If people still insist upon hugging their troubles to themselves, all the charity in the world will not help them. Remember that God is that silent power behind all things, always ready to spring into expression when we have provided the proper channels, which are receptive and positive faith in the evidence of things not seen with the physical eye but eternal in the heavens.

You have probably said more than once, "I was sure this was going to happen." Was it a premonition or things happened that way because of your thoughts? Think about several events that occurred in your life, and try to remember what kind of thoughts were in your mind, before the event took place. You might be surprised to discover that in many instances, there was a correlation between your thoughts and the event. This might seem strange to you, but thoughts have power.

The thoughts that we often repeat in our mind influence our behavior and attitude, our actions and reactions, as well as our life and the people around us. As our thoughts are, so is our life. This means that we need to be careful with our thoughts, especially with thoughts that we repeat often. One thought is not powerful enough to make change in our life. However, if we repeat the same thought frequently, it will gain power, become stronger and affect our life.

THE ACTUAL BATTLE WITH THE DEVIL

The devil do not hate Man but positive change, why the devil is considered man's enemy is that, man was originally created to be positive, which is what the devil hates and is trying everything possible to frustrate. That is why any man who's positively minded has the devil to content with because the devil plans and influences the world with evil to make man create evil. Mind you the devil lacks the ability to create, or make neither positive nor negative change, but totally depends on man for execution of his plans to make negative creations. The devil influences man to invent or create negative impact. Man is the only Creator.

It has been acknowledged previously, that the fall of man came as a result of ignorance; ignorance remains the greatest weak point of every living man, the advantage which the devil used against man in the beginning was his knowledge of the truth which man was ignorant of. The devil hunts every day after men who lacks understanding to use them to accomplish his purpose which will always be different from their original purpose.

POSITIVE CHANGE

We must purposefully set our faces to the rising consciousness of truth. Making positive change is never easy; anyone who says it's easy lacks the truth. Though it is not easy but we are mean to face it because we are strong enough, knowing that life is not about waiting for the storms to pass, it's about learning how to dance in the rain. An attitude of positive expectation is the mark of the superior personality. All that is in any way negative must be wiped off the slate and we must daily come into the higher thought, to be washed clean of the dust and chaos of the objective life. In the silence of the soul's communion with the Great Cause of All Being, into the stillness of the Absolute, into the secret place of the Most High, back of the din and the ceaseless roar of life, we shall find a resting place and a place of real spiritual power. Speak in this inner silence and say, "I am one with the Almighty; I am one with all life, with all power, with all presence.

Here we make known all our needs and wants, and here we receive first hand from the Infinite all that we shall ever need to make life healthy, happy and harmonious. Few enter here, because of the belief that conditions and circumstances control. Know that there is no law but God's law which is the truth of nature; that the soul sets its own law in the Infinite and that our slightest wish is honored of the Father Mind. Daily practice the truth and daily die to all error-thought. Spend more time receiving and realizing the, presence of the Most High and less time worrying. Wonderful power will come to the one who believes and trusts in that Power in which he has come to believe. Know that all good and all God is with you; All Life and All Power; and never again say, "I fear," but always, "I trust, because 'I know in whom I have believed.'"

POSITIVITY FOR PROSPERITY

Suppose that you are doing a mail order business and sending out cards to the whole country. Take the cards into your hands, or simply think of them and declare into the only Mind that they will accomplish that for which they are sent out; know that every word written on them is truth and carries its own conviction with it; see them each reaching that place where it will be received with gladness and read with interest; declare this to be so now; feel it to be the truth; mentally assert that each card will find its way to the exact place where it will be wanted and where it will benefit the receiver; feel that each card is cared for by the Spirit; that it is a messenger of truth and power and that it will carry conviction and realization with it.

When the word is spoken always feel that Mind at once takes it up and never fails to act upon it. Our place in the creative order is to know this and to be willing to do all that we can without hurry or worry, and, above all else, to trust absolutely in the Spirit to do the rest. He who sees most clearly and believes most implicitly will make the greatest demonstration. This one should be you, and will be you as soon as the false thought is gone and the realization that there is but the one power and the one presence comes. We are wrapped in an Infinite Love and Intelligence and we should cover ourselves with it and claim its protection from all evil. Declare that your word is the presence and the activity of the Power of all that is and wait for the perfect concept to unfold.

MONEY A SPIRITUAL IDEA

Many people seem to think that money must be evil, although I have never as yet seen any who did not want a lot of this evil in their lives. If all is an expression of life, then money is an expression of life, and as such, must be good. Without a certain amount of it in this life, we would have a hard time. But, how to get it that is the race problem. How shall we acquire wealth? Money didn't make itself, and not being self-creative it must be an effect. Behind it must be the Cause that projects it. That cause is never seen; no cause is ever seen.

Consciousness is cause and people who have a money consciousness have the outward expression of it. People, who have it as a sure reality in their mind, have it as an expression in their pocket. People who don't have this mental likeness don't have money in their pockets. What we need to do is to acquire a money consciousness. This may seem very material, but the true idea of money is not material – it is spiritual. We need to make our unity with it. We can never do this while we hold it away from us by thinking that we haven't it.

Let us change the method and begin to make our unity with supply by daily declaring that all the Power in the

Universe is daily bringing to us all that we can use. Feel the presence of supply. Know that it is yours now.

Make yourself feel that you now have, and to you shall be given. Work with yourself until there is nothing in you that doubts. Money cannot be kept away from the man who understands that all is Mind, and that Divine Law governs his life. Daily give thanks for perfect supply. Feel it to be yours that you have entered into the full possession of it now.

Refuse to talk poverty or limitation. Stick to it that you are rich. Get the million dollar consciousness. There is no other way, and this will react into everything that you do. See money coming to you from every source and from every direction. Know that everything is working for your good. Realize in your life the presence of an Omnipotent Power. Speak forth into it, and feel that it responds to your approach.

Whenever you see anything or anybody whom you think has more than you, at once affirm that you have the same thing. This doesn't mean that you have what is his, but that you have as much. It means that all you need is yours. Whenever you think about anything big, at once say, "That means me." In this way you learn to unify yourself, in the Law, with large concepts, and according to the way that Law works, it will tend to produce that thing for you.

Never let yourself doubt for even a minute. Always be positive about yourself. Keep watch over the inner workings of your thought, and the Law will do the rest.

CONGRATULATIONS! STUDY AND ANALYSE THE NEW YOU, YOU ARE GREAT

THE INSPIRED AUTHORING

CHANGE

EMMANUEL ERIM

CHANGE

EMMANUEL ERIM

TABLE OF CONTENTS

DEDICATION

I specially dedicate this book to my Late Father, Late Mr. Otioh, Ankpo Erim and to my Great Mother, Eld. Mrs. Justina Erim.

ACKNOWLEDGEMENT

I appreciate God for the series of inspirations through which this book has reached its peak.

I also appreciate the Great Enerst Shuttleff Holmes who's "Creative Mind and Success" has contributed immensely to the propagation of this version of his inspired authoring.

As you read ahead, if carefully completed, you will experience 75% change in your general understanding of life, insentiently. This change will surely unleash the real you.

INTRODUCTION

The most mysterious event of life is change, change is either positive or negative, and everything in the world is experiencing change. As insignificant as an element of change it will surely manifest a significant change. Change in all definition is a gradual differentiation with time, which can be traced or noticed.

Change existed in the very beginning of things, and still exist now, we can say that the creation were changes resulting from the commands from the Creator. The command is the action and the result became a change noticeable as creation. Change is continuous and will keep occurring which means that creation is continuous, as the sun's shadow shifts, so there is no permanence on earth. Everything comes to pass, nothing comes to stay, and nothing remains constant except change itself.

Change is the result of a new action. All change is not growth, as all movement is not forward. While all changes do not lead to improvement, all improvement requires change which is why change could be either positive or negative. The ability to develop, test, and implement changes is essential for any individual that wants to continuously improve.

To change means to add to, remove from or make a new one, which implies the same as to create. Whoever has the ability to create, solely, has the ability to change what is created. Everything which exists today was created; we learn that in the beginning when there was nothing, creation started that means change started right from the beginning, everything we see today came as a result of change or creation. The Creator is the only one to continue creation and changing the world without limit to where, how and what to.

THE CREATOR

Let's discover who the Creator is; the Creator is a very sophisticated being. In the hierarchy of power, Almighty God is the most powerful, followed by the Creator. The Creator created the heavens and the earth, the earth was formless and empty, and darkness was over the surface of the deep. The Creator went ahead and created the light and separated it from the darkness, created land and separated it from the waters, created vegetation on the land and aquatic creatures, created the sun, moon and the stars.

Who is now the Creator? This is the question in your mind, but let me hint you. There is no significant difference between Almighty God and the Creator. The Creator is the centre of God in God, the Creator can also be considered as God's companion, being made to be like God. You can now make right deductions of who the Creator is, let's now discover the Creator.

The Creator is man. This book is going to be driving on the sub-theme "The Hidden Power of Man". The Almighty God is not and has no intensions to being the Creator which the truth of nature reveals, creation power is given only to man, to create and change the entire universe without any limit. God only assumed the position of the Creator so as to create a few things that will make man comfortable in a way of showing example to man on what he should do, but after God created man, he stopped creating because creation is not the duty of God but of man, he made man to become the

Creator and continue from where He stopped. Which means that; man is occupying the same office which created the Heavens and the Earth, and which makes man capable of changing and creating anything, all that man needs to do is to understand the truth which is the truth of nature.

Therefore it follows that man, too, is made out of God, since God is all. And as a result, he must partake of God's nature, for we are "made in His image." Man is a center of God in God. Whatever God is universally, man must be in his individual world.

God made man to live with Him, to be one with the Father. Indeed, it is true that those who have felt this most deeply have had a resultant spiritual power that leads us to suppose that God really did make man as a companion. "As the Father hath life within Himself, so hath he given it to the man to have life within himself." Man's mind is made out of God's mind, and all that man is or ever will be, all that he has or ever will have, must partake of the God's nature. Man did not make it so, but it is so, and he must accept the fact and see what he can do with it.

Having the same power in his individual life that God has in the Universal, then this unearthing will imply liberty from all servitude when he understands the truth of nature. As God oversees His Universal world so will man govern his individual world, always subject to the greater law and life. God governs not through physical law as result, but first by inner knowing – then the physical follows. In the same way, man governs his world by the process which we will call, for want of a better name, the power of his thought. Man's inner life is one with the Father.

There is no separation, for the self-evident reason that there is nothing to separate him from God, because there is nothing but life. The separation of two things implies putting a different element between them; but as there is nothing different from God, the unity of God and man is established forever. "My Father and I are One" is a simple statement of a great soul who perceived life as it really is and not from the mere standpoint of outer conditions. Taking as the starting point that man has the same life as God, it follows that he uses the same creative process and changing ability. Everything is one, comes from the same source and returns again to it. “The things which are seen are not made of the things which do appear.” What we see comes from what we do not see.

This explains the observable universe, and is the only possible explanation. As God’s thought makes worlds and peoples in them with all living things, so does our thought make our world and peoples it with all the understandings we have had. By the activity of our thought things come into our life, and we are limited because we have not known the truth; we have thought that outside things controlled us, when all the time we have had that within which could have changed everything and given us freedom from bondage.

Why did God create man and make him a free agent? Isn’t this the question in your mind? If God had created us to conform to, or to be anything that was not of our will, we should not have had individuality at all, we should be automatons. Since we know that we are individuals, we know that God made us thus; and we are just discovering the reason why. Let any man realize this, the greatest truth in all ages, and he will find it will answer all questions. He will be satisfied that things are what they are. He will perceive that he may use his own God-given power so to work, to think and to live that he will in no way hinder the greater law from operating through him.

According to the clearness of his perception and the greatness of his realization of this truth will he provide within himself a starting point through which he may operate. There will no longer be a sense of separation, but in its place will come that divine assurance that he is one with God, and thus will he find his freedom from all suffering, whether it be of body, mind or estate.

The Creator has been revealed to be Man, and Man has ever since inception been fully involved in creation. Man has everything it takes to create whatever man wants, as good Creator as God was, so is man. Man is so equipped enough to create a planet into existence, God has shown man all level of humility and love by allowing man to have all the tools of creation that He possesses which makes man an efficient creator just as God was. The truth of nature says that God created man in His own image and likeness, God had to do this in order for man to be fit enough to be in companion with Him.

The whole universe is waiting and willing to conform to whatever the Creator wants of it. Man being the only Creator as God has made him reserves the power to create and change the entire universe.

Whoever created a computer software/application reserves the right in the form of a source code through which more creation and changes may be effected on the said software/application, except the owner decides to handover the copyrights or source code to another person, which is what was done between God and man. God has given man the right to subdue the earth and he remains the only one with the tools of creation which makes him the only Creator. The Creator of the universe reserves the power and legal right to change the universe; therefore, man alone has the power to change his world.

The power which the Creator uses for creation comes from his ability to understand the truth, any man that lacks understanding of the truth, lacks the creative ability and ceases from his position as the Creator, only men who understand the truth do change the world, add to creation and lead a successful life. Living successfully in this case implies; man's ability to fulfill the purpose for which he existed, man is supposed to dominate and subdue all the creation. The greatest joy of God is in seeing man understand the truth, live by it and fulfill his purpose.

Every man is a completed project, in other words, God Almighty owes man nothing, and man has in him everything he wants, the love of God for man has been perfected by giving man access to God's Divine Nature.

Man needs to know the truth, everything we want is in Him and we have every access to the truth. The fall of man came as a result of ignorance; ignorance remains the greatest weak point of every living man, the advantage which the devil used against man in the beginning was his knowledge of the truth which man was ignorant of. Therefore, the way forward, if man must resume his place as the Creator is to embrace knowledge and forsake ignorance.

WHAT BRINGS ABOUT CHANGE?

NEEDS

All the created things were created as a result of need, which means, everything that was created is needful and important to the world. While needs are universal, desires or wants are temporal, spatial, and personal. Thus, desires can be or actually are manipulated by perverted applications of needs approaches. If this distinction is acceptable, the term 'needs' would stand for general principles of human existence.

Have you ever wondered the importance of some creatures to nature or to the Creator; you need to first understand that everything created by the Creator was created for the Creator's use. Now let's see it from this scenario; the Creator was mean to own the world and everything created and to create more things according to his needs. Also, the Creator is supposed to according to his will change whatever is created to suite his needs. Therefore, seeing needs is one activity which qualifies one to be called Creator, the Creator as implied by this book is another version of man, meaning; a fulfilled version of man. In the circular world they are referred to as leaders, legends in their respective fields, great men, successful men, and so on.

The major factor that is behind and which inspires and drives the Creator into creating anything is need. The ability to conceive a burden or need in heart is always the first step to invention, change and creation. Seeing a need gives you an avenue to ask and we get in life what we have the courage to ask for.

Change begins within, you can change the entire universe just by changing one thing in you, everyone thinks of changing the world, but no one thinks of changing himself. When we are no longer able to change a situation, we are challenged to change ourselves. Conceive a burden and the world stands the risk of changing again.

IDEAS

Conception of new ideas is another factor which brings about change, if an idea is conceived and appreciated; it has the potency to manifest as change. Therefore, conceiving an idea about any realized need which you want to solve is another step taken to ensure change. When you are fed with ideas which are picked up for discussion, exchanged, altered and repeated, or discarded. Ideas get the discourse off the ground and make up its core nourishment.

Though creating ideas is actually a thought process which takes some form in the mind before becoming a reality. There is certainly nothing unsystematic about generating ideas. Some start out in a fantasy form only to be fine-tuned into creating something functional and practical.

If you dream of ever being great, then one thing you should treasure most is ideas, this is what rules the world, this is what makes the rich, and it's a great determinant of success. Inspired ideas are generated in the mind, for creative purpose.

CRITERIA TO MAKE A CHANGE

CHARISMA

There are some qualities which are common among world changers; we shall discuss them in this session. Let's start with the first being charisma, making change in all aspect of life is the hobby of charismatic people, throughout my career I have often found myself in the company of individuals who have that indefinable quality that draws you to them, and leaves you feeling wonderfully energised as a result of meeting them.

Charismatic people became my passion. I paid attention to the way Charismatic people spoke, how they moved, their posture and the type of words they used. The more I noticed the more confused I became about being able to categorise the elements that typify this level of intensive magnetism.

Consequently, I was a victim of an eventual change which came as a result of my involvement with a very charismatic young man. Late In the month of December, 2018, I saw an adverts flyer in Diamond Bank as I went to deposit, I picked interest in meeting the team offering the services as it was in my field (IT Services). They were offering website development & business starters' packages. Two weeks after I contacted them I was lucky to meet with the Chief Executive Officer at Mr. Fans in Calabar, Cross River State of Nigeria.

Before I go any further with how meeting this young man influenced, affected and obviously change me in many ways, let me sound a piece of advice; we all have to be careful with the kind of people we set out for our lives or get attracted to for they have a way of influencing and changing us.

The young man remains anonymous; I loved his approach, the way he spoke, laughed, dressed, walked and everything about him was interesting. He offered me to be a member of his team after several hours of conversation. After a while he invited me to their team meeting, introduced me and offered to be paying me to work for the team as a website developer. As time went on he discovered that I was good in it and had to hand over a very important project of his team to me, and he made me the director of ICT in the team.

Before now, I had a female friend who travelled out of town; she stayed for a month and came back. On meeting me, she stared at me for more than it was necessary and was saying that I have really changed in the way I walked, spoke, laughed and so on. She became very eager to know the secret behind the change, I personally knew the secret, I equally knew when I began changing in the way I spoke and laughed but I couldn't help or prevent it because of how much I really wished to be like him in my mind. Those thought of being like him started manifesting automatically without me doing anything to enhance those changes.

Anything you take to heart has a way of becoming part of you including the people you set out for your live. Charisma is one quality you must possess if you must affect, influence and change your world.

Charismatic people possess a potent blend of attractiveness and presence that commands attention with an irresistible magnetic force.

According to studies of babies and infants by Judith Langlois of the University of Texas, in experimental studies attractive people earn more and progress further in their careers. A Charismatic person doesn't have to be physically attractive to possess the power to attract. Attractiveness is hard wired in our brains and stimulates a primeval reaction from others that 'attractive means they are healthier and have better breeding potential.' When we meet or observe a Charismatic person we are attracted to their aura of 'special-ness', believing that their 'special-ness' could overspill into our own personality, infecting us, as if by osmosis, with a magical presence.

As with all power, possessing Charisma brings with it great responsibility; as you get to grips with the profound ways you can develop and strengthen your

Charisma you'll experience an increase in your personal power. If you use this power with positive intent for others you will be acting from an inner platform of compassion and integrity that will serve to electrify your presence to the next stage. Charisma is a must trait for all world changers, you must possess it if you must affect and change your world.

HOW TO DEVELOP CHARISMA

Life is 10% what happens to us and 90% how we react to it. Any man who knows how to love everybody, no matter who they are, will find ample of people who will return that love to him. This is not mere mawkishness, and it is more than a religious attitude of mind; it is a deep scientific fact, and one to which we should pay attention. The reason is this: As all is mind, and as we attract to us what we first become, until we learn to love we are not sending out love vibrations, and not until we send out love vibrations can we receive love in return.

The first thing to do is to learn to love everybody. If you have not done this, begin now. There is always more good than bad in people, and seeing the good tends to bring it forth. Love is the greatest healing and drawing power on earth. It is the very cause for our being, and that elucidates why it is that people should have something or somebody to love. The life that has not loved has not lived; it is still dead. Love is the sole impulse for creation; and the man who does not have it as the greatest incentive in his life has never developed the real creative instinct.

The whole universe is established upon love. The atmosphere created by a real lover of the race is so powerful that although, his other shortcomings may be many, still the world will love him in return. "To him who loves much, much will be given." People are dying for real human interest, for someone to tell them that they are all right. Which people do we like the better: the one who is always full of trouble and faultfinding, or the one who looks at the world as his friend and loves it?

The question does not need to be asked; we know that we want the company of the person who loves and loving, forgets all else. The only reason we think other people are "queer" is because they do not happen to think as we do. We must get over this little, petty attitude and see things in the large. The person who sees what he wants to see, regardless of what appears, will someday experience in the outer what he has so faithfully seen within.

From egoistic reasons alone, if from no loftier reason, we cannot afford to find fault or to hate or even to hold in mind anything against any living soul. The God who is love cannot hear the prayer of the man who is not love. Love and cooperation will yet be found to be the greatest business principle on earth. "God is Love." We will make our unity with all people, with all life. We will affirm that God in us is unified with God in all. This One is now drawing into our life all love and fellowship. I am one with all people, with all things, with all life. As I listen in the silence the voice of all humanity speaks to me and answers the love that I hold out to it. This great love that I now feel for the world is the love of God, and it is felt by all and returned from all. Nothing comes in between because there is nothing but love to come in between.

I understand all people and that understanding is reflected back to me from all people. I help, therefore I am helped. I uplift, therefore I am uplifted. Nothing can mar this perfect picture of myself and my relations with the world; it is the truth, the whole truth, and nothing but the truth. I am now surrounded by all love, all friendship, all companionship, all health, all happiness, and all success. I am one with life. I wait in the silence while the Great Spirit bears this message to the whole world.

GAIN INDEPENDENCE

God gave us the gift of life; it is up to us to give ourselves the gift of living well. Life isn't about finding yourself, life is about creating yourself. Never depend on other people. You have strength of your own that is great enough to create a very wonderful world around you. The Almighty has implanted a mastermind within the soul of everyone and what we need to do is to unearth that inner genius and cause it to shine forth.

We will never do this while we look to others for direction. “To thine own self repair, wait thou within the silence dim, and thou shalt find Him there.” All the power and intelligence of the Universe is already within, waiting to be utilized. Self-reliance is the word to abide on. Listen to your own voice; it will speak in terms that are unmistakable.

Belief in your own self more than in all else, all great men have learned to do this. Every person, within his own soul, is in direct communication with the Infinite Understanding. When we depend on other people we are simply taking their light and trying to light our path with it. When we depend on ourselves we are depending on that inner voice that is God, speaking in and through man. “Man is the inlet and the outlet to all there is in

God.” God has made us and brought us up to where we recognize our own individuality; from now on we will have to let Him express through us. If it were different we should not be individuals. “Behold I stand at the door and wait.” This is a statement of the near presence of power; but we, the Individual, must open the door. This door is our thought and we are the guardian of it, and when we do open the door we will find that the Divine Presence is right at hand, waiting, ready and willing to do for us all that we can believe. We are strong with the strength of the Infinite. We are not weak. We are great and not mean. We are one with the Infinite Mind.

When you have a real thing to do, keep it to yourself, don’t talk about it. Just know in your own mind what it is that you want and keep still about it. Often when we think that we will do some big thing we begin to talk about it and the first thing we know all the power seems to be gone.

This is what happens. We are all sending out into Mind a constant stream of thought; the clearer it is the better will it manifest; if it becomes doubtful it will not have so clear a manifestation. If it is confused it will manifest only confusion. When you want to do a big thing, get the mental pattern, make it perfect, know just what it means, enlarge your thought, keep it to yourself, pass it over to the creative power behind all things, wait and listen, and when the impression comes, follow it with assurance. Don't talk to anyone about it. Never listen to negative talk or pay any attention to it and you will succeed where all others fail. It takes one man to change the entire universe, it takes only you to create everything your mind can conceive, your mind cannot conceive more than it can execute, so you do not need assistance from anyone to accomplish your dreams.

HARD-WORK

Hard work entails having the strength to do a thing and the perseverance to continue until success is achieved. The most beautiful people I've known are those who have known trials, have known struggles, have known loss, and have found their way out of the depths. Strength does not come from winning. Your struggles develop your strengths. When you go through hardships and decide not to surrender, that is strength. Being hard working is the edge that successful people have over others.

Everyone wants to be successful. Of course, your definition of success can and should be different – because success should mean something different to each of us – but still, we all want to succeed at whatever we choose to do. (Otherwise, why do it?) But whenever I give a thought to how success is often based on outworking other people – both in terms of effort and in terms of hours spent – I get indignant responses. “What about work-life balance?” some ask. “Work smarter, not harder,” others say. Yeah, well, no way.

You can't have it both ways. On the one hand, we celebrate people who have worked incredibly hard and achieved incredible success. They're icons, world changers and are putting in enough to be the Creator which God made them. Take successful entrepreneurs. Bill Gates evidently never slept, never changed clothes, never did anything but code and manoeuvre and strategise. In an industry filled with incredibly smart people – where smart was and is commonplace – he rose to the top by also working incredibly hard.

Mark Cuban didn't take a vacation for seven years while he started his first company. Elon Musk says, "You just have to put in 80- to 100-hour weeks every week. If other people are putting in 40-hour workweeks and you're putting in 100hour workweeks, then, even if you're doing the same thing, you know that you will achieve in four months what it takes them a year to achieve." In fact, the common theme of almost every tale of entrepreneurial success is a person who worked countless 18- to 24-hour days. Replace the names and their stories sound almost identical. Even Tim Ferriss, the lord of the four hour-workweek manor, stays incredibly busy with all his projects. (Of course, to Tim it doesn't feel like work.) Or take successful people in other professions.

Jeffrey Immelt, the chief executive of GE, worked 100-hour weeks for 24 years. In a company filled with incredibly driven people – where incredible drive is commonplace – he rose to the top by also working incredibly hard. Tim Cook of Apple still wants to be first in, last out. Or take sports. Hard work has clearly paid off for all of them. Yet somehow people think hard work won't work for them. Maybe that's because of the whole "work smarter" thing? Successful people already work smarter.
They don't work mindlessly or inefficiently or ineffectively.

Where success is concerned, working smarter is a given. Extremely successful people work smarter and they work harder. Their effort is heroic, their payoff is often legendary, and we celebrate them for it. "Wait," you say. "Luck plays a big part in success. So, does timing. So, do a lot of other factors." You're right. But you can't control luck. You can't always control timing. You can't always control all those other factors. What can you always control? How hard you work. Let's say luck decides to pay everyone with a particular amount which you cannot control, what is going to set the difference and keep you outstanding is the extra effort you put. Again, everyone defines success differently, as well everyone should.

You may not be smarter than everyone else. You may not be as talented. You may not have the same great connections, the same great environment, or the same great education. If you're on the downside of advantage, you may have none of those things. But you can always rely on your courage, your effort, and your perseverance.

You can always substitute effort for skill and experience, secure in the knowledge that, over time, incredible effort will absolutely breed skill and experience. You can always, always, always work harder than everyone else. Want to be different? Hard work can be your immediate difference. Make hard work your favourite words, whether at work or at home or in your marriage or wherever your definition of success takes you. That way you'll never have to look back and wonder what you might have accomplished if only you had tried harder.

The most significant life lesson I have learned from working with Registered Holsteins is that hard work leads to success. Whether you want a political office, entrepreneurial success, marital success, academic success, or whatever you want to change in your world, hard work is inevitable. Keep striving and working harder because there are many ways of going forward, but only one way of standing still.

FAITH

All of the great inventions in the world have been accomplished by people who have kept on trying when there seemed to be no hope at all.

Faith is necessary always when we want something we must believe. Faith is not in asking for something but it is in believing that we already have the things that we need. This already-believing is necessary because all is mind, and until we have provided that full acceptance, we have not made a mold into which mind could pour itself and through which it could manifest.

In the previous chapters, we made mentioned that man has access to God's Divine Nature, through which the heavens and the earth was created. God made man to be the Creator of all things including what is considered impossible that man can make anything through faith.

This positive belief is absolutely essential to real creative work; and if we do not at present have it, then we must develop it. All is law, and cause and effect obtain through all life. Mind is cause, and what we term matter, or the visible, is effect. As water will freeze into the form that it is poured, so mind will solidify only into the forms that our thought takes. Thought is form. The individual provides the form; he never creates or even manifests, – that is, of himself; there is something that does all this for him. His sole activity is the use of this power.

This authority is always at hand ready to be spoken into and at once ready to form the words into visible expression. But the mold that most of us provide is a very poor one, and we change it so quickly that it is more like a motion picture than anything else. Already we have the power; it is the gift of the Most High in its Finite Expression. But our ignorance of its use has caused us to create the wrong form, which in its turn has caused mind to produce the form which we have thought into it. From this truth of nature or law of cause and effect we may never hope to escape; and while we may think of it as a hard thing, at first, yet, when we understand, we shall see it as absolute justice without which there could be no real self-acting, individual life at all.

Because of our divine individuality, even God may have to wait our recognition of the truth. People in business will do well to remember this and so to form their thought that they will be willing to receive what they send out. No thought of discouragement or disorder should ever be created, but only positive assurance, strong thoughts of success, of Divine activity, the feeling that through understanding the truth of nature all things are possible, the belief that we are One with that Great Mind. These are the thoughts that make for success. The realization that we are dealing with one and not with two powers enables us to think with clearness.

We are not troubled about competition or opposition or failure because there is nothing but life, and this life is continually giving to us all that we could ask for, wish, or think into it. We can now see how essential it is that thought should be held one-pointed; that we should think always and only upon what we want, never letting our mind dwell on anything else. In this way the Spirit works through us.

Faith is the only currency that is a legal tender and accepted across the globe. When money fails, faith never fails. It's only faith that can draw from the reserves of Heaven. Faith comes by revelation; the truth of nature says “So then faith cometh by hearing, and hearing and understanding the truth.” The first level is reading, the second level is revelation.

What Is Faith? It is putting the truth to work. Taking steps on the truth you have learned. Obeying the truth of nature to prove that you believe in the Divine Nature, redemption is a call to profitable living.

NATURE'S DEBT STATUS

Nature is not and will never be indebted to the Creator; nature pays the Creator exactly what the Creator banks within it. Nature was created by and subjected to the Creator and at such cannot disobey the Creator; everything that The Creator has is what he has created into and through nature. The Creator only needs an understanding of the truth in order to manipulate nature; the same degree of the power of creation which existed is still in existence.

TOOLS FOR CHANGE/CREATION

THE TRUTH OF NATURE

Never does nature say one thing and wisdom another. Therefore knowing the truth about nature is having wisdom. The Creator must realize that he has life within himself as the great gift of God to him. If he really has life, if it is the same nature as the life of God, if he is an individual and has the right of self-choice which constitutes individuality; then it follows that he can do with his life what the wants to do: he can make out of Himself that which he wishes. Liberty is his, but this liberty is within law and never outside it, the law is the truth of nature. The Creator must have understanding of the truth.

The Creator is always in immediate connection with the Infinite of understanding. We are immersed in a living intelligence; we are surrounded by a Power that knows, for "In Him we live and move and have our being." If our outer thought were never confused, we should at all times draw from this Infinite source of knowledge; we should be guided by It and never make mistakes; our minds would be like the smooth surface of a lake, unruffled by wind and storm.

The truth of nature is the Word of God through which creation was perfected, the one important tool through which creation was established is the Word of God which is the truth of nature. In the beginning was the word and the word was with God and the word was God, He was in the beginning with God, all things were made through Him and without Him nothing was made that was made.

The most efficient tool of creation remains the word of truth, the truth of nature which is in God and has been revealed to be God. Therefore, knowing the truth is same as knowing God, having faith in the truth is also having faith in God. This tool is for creation and has been handed over to the Creator, that through it, the Creator shall fulfill His purpose.

The Creator's word, spoken forth through creative mind, is endowed with power of manifestation. "By our words we are justified and by our words we are condemned."

Our word has the exact amount of power that we put into it. This does not mean power through effort or strain but power through absolute conviction, or faith. It is like a little messenger who knows what he is doing and knows just how to do it. We speak into our words the intelligence which we are, and backed by that greater intelligence of the Universal Mind our word becomes a law unto the thing for which it is spoken.

If any word has power it means that all words have power. Some words may have more power than others, according to our faith, but all words have some power. How careful, then, we should be what kind of words we are speaking for creation is perfected through the words of the Creator.

All this goes to prove that we really are one with the Infinite Mind, and that our words have the power of life within them; that the word is always with us and never far off. The word is within our own mouth. Every time we speak we are using power, we are creating and changing the world. We are one in mind with the whole universe; we are all eternally united in this mind with real power. It is our own fault if we do not use this truth after we see it. We should feel ourselves surrounded by this mind, this great pulsating life, this all-seeing and all-knowing reality.

When we do feel this near presence, this great power and life, then all we have to do is to speak forth into it, speak with all the positive conviction of the soul that has found its source, and above all else never fear but that it will be done unto us even as we have believed. What wonderful power, what a newness of life and of power of expression, is waiting for those who really believe. What may the race not attain to when men wake up to the real facts of being? As yet the race has not begun to live, but the time is drawing near. Already thousands are using this great power, and thousands are eagerly watching and waiting for the new day.

Understanding wisdom is the key. Wisdom is in the truth of nature, so, and understanding natural truth is having wisdom. An inquiry into Truth is an inquiry into the cause of things as the human race sees and experiences them. The truth of nature is a very important tool for creation and the Creator must acknowledge this for all level of efficiency.

THE MIND

The mind is the centre of it all and the starting point of our thought must always begin with our understandings. We all know that life is, else we could not even think that we are. Since we can think, say and feel we must be. We live, we are conscious of life; therefore we must be and life must be. If we are life and mindfulness (self-knowing) then it means that we must have come from life and mindfulness. Let us start, then, with this simple fact: Life is and life is conscious.

But what is the nature of this life; is it physical, mental, material or spiritual? A little careful thinking based upon logic, more than any merely personal opinion, will do much in clearing up some of these questions that at first seem to stagger us with their bigness. How much of that which is may we call life? The answer would have to be: Life is all that there is; it is the reason for all that we see, hear, feel-- all that we experience in any way.

Now nothing from nothing leaves anything, and it is impossible for something to proceed from nothing. Since something is, that from which it came must be all that is. Life, then, is all that there is. Everything comes from it, we included. The next question is, how do things come from life? How do the things that we see come from the things that we do not see? The things that we see must be real because we see them. To say they are not real will never explain them nor answer any question about them. God's world is not a world of illusion but one of divine realities. The truth must not explain away things that we see.

It must explain what they are. We are living and experiencing varying degrees of consciousness and conditions. Only when the why of this living and of our experiences is understood will we know the least thing about the truth.

OUR LIFE IS A RESULT OF OUR THINKING

It is easy for the ordinary person to see how it is that mind can control, and to a certain extent govern, the functions of the body. Some can go even further than this and see that the body is governed entirely by mindfulness. This they can see without much difficulty, but it is not so easy for them to see how it is that thought governs their conditions and decides whether they are to be successes or failures. Here we will stop to ask the question: If our conditions are not controlled by thought, by what, then, are they controlled? Some will say that conditions are controlled by circumstances. But what are circumstances? Are they "cause" or are they "effect?" Of course they are always effect; everything that we see is an effect. An effect is something that follows a cause, and we are dealing with causation only; effects do not make themselves, but they are held in place by mind, or causation.

If this does not answer your thought, begin over again and realize that behind everything that is seen is the silent cause. In your life you are that cause. There is nothing but mind, and nothing moves except as mind moves it. We have agreed that, while God is love, yet your life is governed absolutely by mind, or law. In our lives of conditions we are the cause, and nothing moves except as our mind moves it. The activity of our mind is thought. We are always acting because we are always thinking.

At all times we are either drawing things to us or we are pushing them away from us. In the ordinary individual this process goes on without his ever knowing it consciously, but ignorance of the law will excuse no one from its effects. “What?” someone will say, “Do you think that I thought failure or wanted to fail?” Of course not. You would be foolish to think that; but according to the law which we cannot deny, you must have thought things that would produce failure. Perhaps you thought that failure might come, or in some other way you gave it entrance to your mind.

Thinking back over the reason for things, you will find that you are surrounded by a mind, or law that casts back at the thinker manifested, everything that he thinks. If this were not true, the Creator would not be an individual. Individuality can mean only the ability to think what we want to think. If that thought is to have power in our lives then there has to be something that will manifest it.

No matter what we may do, law will always obtain. If we are thinking of ourselves as poor and needy, then mind has no choice but to return what we have thought into it. At first this may be hard to realize, but the truth will reveal to the seeker that law could act in no other way.

Whatever we think is the pattern, and mind is the builder. The Master, realizing this law, said, "It is done unto you even as you have believed." Shall we doubt but that this great Way Shower knew what he was talking about? Did He not say, "It is done unto you"? What a wonderful thought. "It is done unto you." Nothing to worry about. "It is done unto you." With a tremendous grasp of the power of true spiritual thought, the Master even called forth bread from the ethers of life, and at no time did He ever fail to demonstrate that when one knows the truth he is freed by that knowledge.

Is it any wonder that the truth of nature says, "With all thy getting get understanding"? The Master understood all this, and so it was no more effort for Him to do what

He did than it is for us to breathe or to digest our food. He understood, that is all, because the Master did understand and did use these great laws with objective mindfulness.

The Creator uses creative power that already is. Relatively speaking, he is the creative power in his own life; and so far as his thought goes, there is something that goes with it that has the power to bring forth into manifestation the thing thought of. Hitherto we have used this creative power in ignorance and so have brought upon ourselves all kinds of conditions, but today hundreds of thousands are beginning to use these great laws of their being in a conscious, constructive way. Herein lies the great secret of the New Thought movements under their various names and cults and orders.

All are using the same law even though some deny to others the real revelation. We should get into an attitude of mind wherein we should recognize the truth wherever we may find it. The trouble with most of us is that unless we see sugar in a sugar bowl we think it must be something else, and so we stick to our petty prejudices instead of looking after principles.

WHAT TO DO FIRST

The first thing to realize is that since any thought manifests it means that all thought does the same, else how should we know that the particular thought we were thinking would be the one that would create? Mind must cast back all or none. Just as the creative power of the soil receives all seeds put into it, and at once begins to work upon them, so mind must receive all thought and at once begin to operate upon it. Thus we find that all thought has some power in our lives and over our conditions.

We are making our situations by the creative power of our thought. This atmosphere decides what is to be drawn to it. For instance, you never saw a successful man who went around with an atmosphere of failure. Successful people think about success. A successful man is filled with that understated something which permeates everything that he does with an atmosphere of confidence and strength. In the presence of some people we feel as though nothing were too great to undertake; we are hoisted; we are inspired to do great things, to accomplish; we feel strong, steady, sure. What a power we feel in the presence of big souls, strong men, and noble women! Did you ever stop to inquire why it is that such persons have this kind of an effect over you while others seem to depress, to drag you down, and in their presence you feel as though life were a weight to carry? One type is positive, the other negative. In every physical respect they are just alike, but one has a mental and spiritual power which the other does not have, and without that power the individual can hope to do but little.

Which of these two do we like most? With which do we want to associate? Certainly not with the one that depresses us; we have enough of that already. What about the man who inspires us with our own value? He remains the man we will turn to every time. Before ever we reach him, in our haste to be near, even to hear his voice, do we not feel a strength coming to meet us? Do you think that this man who has such a wonderful power of attraction will ever want for friends? Will he ever have to look up a position? Already so many positions are open to him that he is weighing in his mind which one to take. He does not have to become a success; he already is a success. Thoughts of failure, limitation or poverty are negative and must be counted out of our lives for all time. Somebody will say, “But what of the poor; what are you going to do with them; are they to be left without help?” No; a thousand times no. The same power is in them that is in all men. They will always be poor until they awake and realize what life is. All the charity on earth has never done away with poverty, and never will; if it could have done so it would have done so; it could not, therefore it has not.

It will do a man a thousand times more good to show him how to succeed than it will to tell him he needs charity. We need not listen to all the catastrophe howlers. Let them howl if it does them any good. God has given us the power to create more and change our world and we must use it. We can do more toward saving the world by proving this law than all that charity has ever given it. Right here, in the manifold world today, there is more money and provision than the world can use. Not even a fraction of the wealth of the world is used. Inventors and discoverers are adding to this wealth every day; they are the real people, the great men, the Creators, etc. But in the midst of plenty, surrounded by all the gifts of heaven, man sits and begs for his daily bread. He should be taught to realize that he has brought these conditions upon himself; that instead of blaming God, man or the devil for the circumstances by which he is surrounded, he should learn to seek the truth, to let the dead bury their dead.

We should tell every man who will believe what his real nature is; show him how to overcome all limitations; give him courage; show him the way. If he will not believe, if he will not walk in the way, it is not our fault, and having done all we can, we must go our way. We may sympathize with people but never with trouble, limitation or misery. If people still insist upon hugging their troubles to themselves, all the charity in the world will not help them. Remember that God is that silent power behind all things, always ready to spring into expression when we have provided the proper channels, which are receptive and positive faith in the evidence of things not seen with the physical eye but eternal in the heavens.

You have probably said more than once, “I was sure this was going to happen.” Was it a premonition or things happened that way because of your thoughts? Think about several events that occurred in your life, and try to remember what kind of thoughts were in your mind, before the event took place. You might be surprised to discover that in many instances, there was a correlation between your thoughts and the event. This might seem strange to you, but thoughts have power.

The thoughts that we often repeat in our mind influence our behavior and attitude, our actions and reactions, as well as our life and the people around us. As our thoughts are, so is our life. This means that we need to be careful with our thoughts, especially with thoughts that we repeat often. One thought is not powerful enough to make change in our life. However, if we repeat the same thought frequently, it will gain power, become stronger and affect our life.

THE ACTUAL BATTLE WITH THE DEVIL

The devil do not hate Man but positive change, why the devil is considered man's enemy is that, man was originally created to be positive, which is what the devil hates and is trying everything possible to frustrate. That is why any man who's positively minded has the devil to content with because the devil plans and influences the world with evil to make man create evil. Mind you the devil lacks the ability to create, or make neither positive nor negative change, but totally depends on man for execution of his plans to make negative creations. The devil influences man to invent or create negative impact. Man is the only Creator.

It has been acknowledged previously, that the fall of man came as a result of ignorance; ignorance remains the greatest weak point of every living man, the advantage which the devil used against man in the beginning was his knowledge of the truth which man was ignorant of. The devil hunts every day after men who lacks understanding to use them to accomplish his purpose which will always be different from their original purpose.

POSITIVE CHANGE

We must purposefully set our faces to the rising consciousness of truth. Making positive change is never easy; anyone who says it's easy lacks the truth. Though it is not easy but we are mean to face it because we are strong enough, knowing that life is not about waiting for the storms to pass, it's about learning how to dance in the rain. An attitude of positive expectation is the mark of the superior personality. All that is in any way negative must be wiped off the slate and we must daily come into the higher thought, to be washed clean of the dust and chaos of the objective life. In the silence of the soul's communion with the Great Cause of All Being, into the stillness of the Absolute, into the secret place of the Most High, back of the din and the ceaseless roar of life, we shall find a resting place and a place of real spiritual power. Speak in this inner silence and say, "I am one with the Almighty; I am one with all life, with all power, with all presence.

Here we make known all our needs and wants, and here we receive first hand from the Infinite all that we shall ever need to make life healthy, happy and harmonious. Few enter here, because of the belief that conditions and circumstances control. Know that there is no law but God's law which is the truth of nature; that the soul sets its own law in the Infinite and that our slightest wish is honored of the Father Mind. Daily practice the truth and daily die to all error-thought. Spend more time receiving and realizing the, presence of the Most High and less time worrying. Wonderful power will come to the one who believes and trusts in that Power in which he has come to believe. Know that all good and all God is with you; All Life and All Power; and never again say, "I fear," but always, "I trust, because 'I know in whom I have believed.'"

POSITIVITY FOR PROSPERITY

Suppose that you are doing a mail order business and sending out cards to the whole country. Take the cards into your hands, or simply think of them and declare into the only Mind that they will accomplish that for which they are sent out; know that every word written on them is truth and carries its own conviction with it; see them each reaching that place where it will be received with gladness and read with interest; declare this to be so now; feel it to be the truth; mentally assert that each card will find its way to the exact place where it will be wanted and where it will benefit the receiver; feel that each card is cared for by the Spirit; that it is a messenger of truth and power and that it will carry conviction and realization with it.

When the word is spoken always feel that Mind at once takes it up and never fails to act upon it. Our place in the creative order is to know this and to be willing to do all that we can without hurry or worry, and, above all else, to trust absolutely in the Spirit to do the rest. He who sees most clearly and believes most implicitly will make the greatest demonstration. This one should be you, and will be you as soon as the false thought is gone and the realization that there is but the one power and the one presence comes. We are wrapped in an Infinite Love and Intelligence and we should cover ourselves with it and claim its protection from all evil. Declare that your word is the presence and the activity of the Power of all that is and wait for the perfect concept to unfold.

MONEY A SPIRITUAL IDEA

Many people seem to think that money must be evil, although I have never as yet seen any who did not want a lot of this evil in their lives. If all is an expression of life, then money is an expression of life, and as such, must be good. Without a certain amount of it in this life, we would have a hard time. But, how to get it that is the race problem. How shall we acquire wealth? Money didn't make itself, and not being self-creative it must be an effect. Behind it must be the Cause that projects it. That cause is never seen; no cause is ever seen.

Consciousness is cause and people who have a money consciousness have the outward expression of it. People, who have it as a sure reality in their mind, have it as an expression in their pocket. People who don't have this mental likeness don't have money in their pockets. What we need to do is to acquire a money consciousness. This may seem very material, but the true idea of money is not material – it is spiritual. We need to make our unity with it. We can never do this while we hold it away from us by thinking that we haven't it.

Let us change the method and begin to make our unity with supply by daily declaring that all the Power in the Universe is daily bringing to us all that we can use. Feel the presence of supply. Know that it is yours now.

Make yourself feel that you now have, and to you shall be given. Work with yourself until there is nothing in you that doubts. Money cannot be kept away from the man who understands that all is Mind, and that Divine Law governs his life. Daily give thanks for perfect supply. Feel it to be yours that you have entered into the full possession of it now.

Refuse to talk poverty or limitation. Stick to it that you are rich. Get the million dollar consciousness. There is no other way, and this will react into everything that you do. See money coming to you from every source and from every direction. Know that everything is working for your good. Realize in your life the presence of an Omnipotent Power. Speak forth into it, and feel that it responds to your approach.

Whenever you see anything or anybody whom you think has more than you, at once affirm that you have the same thing. This doesn't mean that you have what is his, but that you have as much. It means that all you need is yours. Whenever you think about anything big, at once say, "That means me." In this way you learn to unify yourself, in the Law, with large concepts, and according to the way that Law works, it will tend to produce that thing for you.

Never let yourself doubt for even a minute. Always be positive about yourself. Keep watch over the inner workings of your thought, and the Law will do the rest.

CONGRATULATIONS! STUDY AND ANALYSE THE NEW YOU, YOU ARE GREAT

www.ingramcontent.com/pod-product-compliance
Ingram Content Group UK Ltd.
Pitfield, Milton Keynes, MK11 3LW, UK
UKHW041942190726
13854UKWH00004B/1746